Meet
Hillary Rodham Clinton

by Valerie Spain

A Bullseye Biography

Random House 🏠 **New York**

With much love to Nicholas and Evan

Photo credits: AP/Wide World Photos, pages 4, 7, 8, 20, 26, 37, 40, 41, 56, 59, 68, 72, 79, 80, 83, 89; Little Rock Convention and Visitors Bureau, page 63; Main South High School, page 31; Reuters/Bettman, pages 11, 13, 14, 66, 74, 81, 86, 92; UPI/Bettman, pages 1, 29, 36; Wellesley College, pages 32, 38, 43, 44, 47, 48, 54; Yale Law School, pages 51, 53.

A BULLSEYE BOOK PUBLISHED BY RANDOM HOUSE, INC.
Cover design by Fabia Wargin Design and Creative Media Applications, Inc.
Copyright © 1994 by Valerie Spain.
All rights reserved under International and Pan-American Copyright Conventions.
Published in the United States by Random House, Inc., New York, and simultaneously in Canada by Random House of Canada Limited, Toronto.
Library of Congress Cataloging-in-Publication Data
Spain, Valerie.
Meet Hillary Rodham Clinton / by Valerie Spain
p. cm. — (A Bullseye biography)
ISBN 0-679-85089-9 (pbk.) — ISBN 0-679-95089-3 (lib. bdg.)
1. Clinton, Hillary Rodham—Juvenile literature. 2. Presidents' spouses—United States—Biography—Juvenile literature. 3. Clinton, Bill, 1946-—Juvenile literature. [1. Clinton, Hillary Rodham. 2. First ladies.
3. Clinton, Bill, 1946- .] I. Title. II. Series.
E887.C55S63 1994 973.929'092—dc20 [B] 93-29194

Manufactured in the United States of America 10 9 8 7 6 5 4 3 2 1

Contents

Bill and Hillary exchange a hug at the Old State House in Little Rock, Arkansas, in celebration of their victory in the presidential election.

1

Victory!

"Hillary! Hillary!" chants the crowd as the new president, Bill Clinton, begins to read his acceptance speech. The platform in front of the Governor's Mansion is surrounded by cheering, clapping people. They have waited hours to see the new First Couple. They have cheered their new president, but they aren't finished yet.

"Hillary! Hillary!" they roar.

Grinning, Bill Clinton says, "It's okay. You can cheer for her too." And he steps back.

A smiling Hillary comes forward. She waves to the crowd. Someone calls out to her, and she throws back her head and laughs loudly. The full, deep laugh that's her trademark. Then she moves back to stand alongside the president. Because he has a sore throat, it is difficult for him to speak. Hillary helps by carefully handing him his notecards.

Now and then, she takes a quick look at the crowd. She thinks, "It's incredible! We've won! We're going to the White House!"

She remembers her meetings with other First Ladies. She wanted to know what the job was like for them. She met with Jacqueline Kennedy Onassis, Lady Bird Johnson, and Rosalynn Carter. Each woman had had her pet projects and interests in the White House.

Jackie was elegant and was well known

Two famous First Ladies: Jacqueline Kennedy wears her trademark pillbox hat; Lady Bird Johnson helps to plant a tree.

Rosalynn Carter on a diplomatic tour of Latin America. Eleanor Roosevelt devoted much of her life to working for children. Here she pours milk for a group of youngsters.

for her wonderful sense of style. Her special interest was redecorating the White House. She searched for antique furniture used by earlier presidents. She even found antique wallpaper to put up in some of the rooms!

Lady Bird Johnson loved gardening and wildflowers. She began flower-planting projects across the country. Her beautification projects continue to give people pleasure.

Rosalynn Carter was an active First Lady and her husband's close adviser. She traveled to foreign countries as his ambassador.

Hillary Clinton has also read about First Ladies throughout history. One of her favorites is Eleanor Roosevelt. Some have said that Hillary's work for children and families is similar to Mrs. Roosevelt's. Hillary's reply to that is, "Those are big shoes to fill!"

But she has the energy to fill them. She

has said many times, "I want to be a voice for children." Now that voice will be heard across the nation, and it will come from the White House.

On this election night, the country has high hopes for Hillary Clinton as well as for the president. They want to see her work for children and families, as she promised. As one man said to her while she was still campaigning, "When you get to the White House, don't forget what you said along the way!"

Hillary grabbed his hand and said, "Oh, I won't! I won't!"

Finally the president finishes his speech. The crowd cheers and surges toward the platform to shake hands. The speakers blare "Don't Stop Thinking About Tomorrow," the theme song of the Clinton campaign. Chelsea Clinton whispers something to her

Children and children's issues have always been important to Hillary Rodham Clinton.

mother. Hillary laughs and hugs her thirteen-year-old daughter. But as she pushes back her daughter's thick hair, she frowns for a moment.

Hillary worries about how Chelsea will deal with the pressures of being the president's daughter. The nation's only First Kid! She has worked hard to give Chelsea a normal childhood, despite their public lives.

During the campaign, Chelsea stayed in Little Rock, Arkansas, with her grandparents. Hillary flew home once a week to be with her. And she rarely missed one of Chelsea's dance performances or softball games.

The Clintons were strict about keeping Chelsea out of the campaign spotlight. They were so strict, in fact, that many people didn't even know the Clintons had a child! So, to introduce her to the nation, Chelsea

Chelsea Clinton shares the spotlight with her parents and Vice-President-elect Al Gore on Election Night.

was allowed to appear in public a few times. But mostly she went quietly to school in Little Rock.

Hillary may worry about Chelsea's future, but is she worried about her own? Challenge

The First Family-elect waves a last good-bye to the crowd in Little Rock as they leave for the inauguration in Washington D.C.

seems only to make her dig in her heels and work harder. Where does she get her strength and drive? Growing up, Hillary had parents who loved her. And a mom who believed in her. A mom who was sure her daughter could do anything she wanted to do.

2

Girlhood Lessons

Hillary and her family had just moved to Park Ridge, Illinois, from their small apartment in Chicago. Four-year-old Hillary was very excited about the move. Everyone said it was nicer in the suburbs. More trees, lots of terrific kids to play with. Well, the trees were pretty, but not all the kids were terrific.

One day Hillary went out to make some new friends. Pigtails swinging, she met a group of boys with a girl in the lead. The girl's name was Suzy.

"Hi," said Hillary. But Suzy wasn't interested in making friends. She gave Hillary a bloody nose instead! Suzy sent Hillary home crying every day after that. Until one day her mom said: "There's no room for cowards in this house. The next time she hits you, I want you to hit her back!"

Hillary gave that some thought. The next day she ran into Suzy again. This time little Hillary closed her eyes and swung her fist. Whack! Suzy went down. The boys stared in amazement. Hillary ran home, yelling, "Mom! I can play with boys now!"

"I had great confidence in that child," her mother said.

Hillary Rodham was the oldest of three children. She was the only girl. Her brothers, Hugh and Tony, adored her. They lived on a quiet, tree-lined street in a brick house on the corner of Elm and Weisner.

Her father, Hugh Rodham, Sr., was in the drapery business. He sold curtains. Dorothy

Rodham was a full-time mom and home-maker. It was a close, loving family, and all the kids had chores: raking leaves, mowing the lawn, shoveling snow. No one got an allowance. Chores were part of what you did for the family.

Brother Tony once joked to a reporter, "Maybe you'd get an extra potato at dinner."

Hugh, Sr., and Dorothy believed in working hard and getting a good education. They wanted their children to excel in school. But as parents they were very different.

Every time Hillary brought home a good report card, she would proudly show her dad. He'd say, "You must go to an easy school."

Hillary was a good student. She always came home with good grades. Her father was tough and demanding, and he always said the same thing. But it didn't bother Hillary! She just worked harder.

She remembers: "My father often said, 'You did well, but could you do better?' I always felt challenged. I always felt there was something else out there I could reach for."

Dorothy Rodham was different. She was a warm, wise, funny lady. She gave her daughter a sense that she could do anything she wanted. And often she set the example. Dorothy hadn't gone to college, but when her children got older, she did go back to school. She studied philosophy.

"For the fun of it," she said.

She had big plans for her daughter.

"I was disappointed Hillary wasn't the first woman on the Supreme Court. But Sandra Day O'Connor beat her to it," Dorothy Rodham once said, laughing.

She raised her children in the 1950s. This

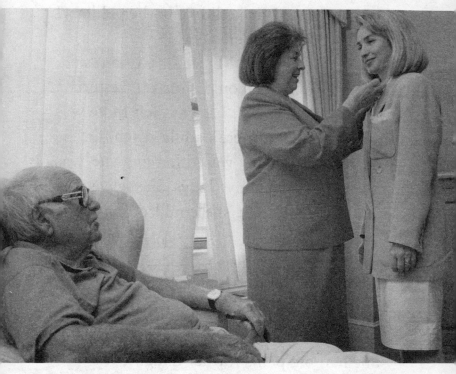

Hillary gets a little help from her mom while her dad looks on during the presidential campaign.

was a time when girls were expected to grow up to be stay-at-home mothers, or maybe teachers or nurses. Dorothy Rodham felt things should be different.

"It seemed to me you should not be held down because you were a girl," she said. "I was determined that no daughter of mine was going to have to be afraid to say what was on her mind."

Perhaps that's why Hillary could stand up to her father's gruff and teasing style of encouragement. She had a mother who believed in her and told her so.

But Hillary didn't need much prodding to do well. She did well at school, in Girl Scouts, at whatever she set her mind to. She had many friends, both girls and boys. She was often the leader, because people liked and trusted her.

As a teen Hillary became involved in the family church, First United Methodist. She joined the youth group right before high school. It might have been a typical round of hikes, picnics, and softball games, if not for one man, the Reverend Don Jones. He was

First United Methodist's new youth minister. He arrived in 1962, fresh from the wide world beyond cozy little Park Ridge. The world was changing. A young and energetic Don Jones brought that change with him. Hillary and the First United Methodist Church would never be the same.

3
Teen Years

The bus pulled up to a recreation center on Chicago's South Side. A lively group of teenagers spilled out. Some carried guitars, and all were excited and nervous. This was their first trip to the city without their parents. Reverend Jones walked ahead of them and shook hands with a tall black gentleman. This man and the young minister had arranged a meeting of city and suburban teenagers of different races, from different worlds.

The laughter of the black teens died away

as the Park Ridge youth group filed into the meeting room. The silence stretched on. Everyone felt awkward. Then Reverend Jones told one of the girls to play her guitar. He walked around the room handing out the words to the songs.

Singing relaxed everyone. Jones had popular songs, folk songs, and songs of freedom from the black civil rights movement. Soon everyone was singing joyfully. After the singing they discussed the words. Many had never thought about the words before.

This was how Don Jones taught the religious ideas of peace, justice, and love. He brought them alive through songs, art, and films.

Every Sunday night, the young people from First United Methodist came together to sing, talk, and pray. Sometimes the Reverend Jones arranged field trips like the one to the recreation center. Always he was testing them, daring them to ask questions about what they saw in the world around them. And while he took the group on serious trips, he also arranged camp retreats. They spent time swimming in the summer and skiing in the winter.

Hillary's first summer job awakened an interest in children. She remembers: "Every morning at about eight o'clock I would fill a red wagon with sports supplies. I pulled it two miles to this little park. From nine until twelve I would watch the small children and play with them. I just loved it. I guess I've been interested in children ever since."

Helping children was also a part of the mission of her church.

"Migrant workers were a big cause in our church," her brother Tony once said. "Hillary would organize carnivals and games. Then we'd participate and raise money for them."

Migrant families work the fields on a farm in California.

When Hillary was growing up, there were still farms just beyond Park Ridge. As they do now, farmers hired people to help harvest their crops. These people are called migrant workers because they migrate, or move, to wherever there is harvesting work to be done. Hillary saw whole families work the fields. Their houses were shacks with no running water or electricity. The migrant children rarely went to school, because as soon as they were old enough they worked in the fields. There were few people around to take care of the infants and toddlers.

With the help of Don Jones, Hillary and a friend organized a baby-sitting brigade. Young people took turns caring for the babies. This was a project Hillary kept going even after Jones left First United Methodist Church.

In high school Hillary was involved in theater, softball, and school government. She loved organizing people and events.

Her physical education teacher remembers, "Kids looked up to her because she was interested in them. She liked people a lot."

Don Jones left First United Methodist Church after Hillary's sophomore year, but not before he took the youth group to Chicago again. This time it was to the Sunday Evening Club at Chicago's Orchestra Hall. The great civil rights leader, Dr. Martin Luther King, Jr., was speaking.

After his speech, the young minister ushered his teens backstage. It was crowded, but Jones caught Dr. King's attention. He brought the civil rights leader over to meet the group from Park Ridge. The kids were wide-eyed. One by one, Jones introduced them to Dr. King. Hillary was barely able to stay still as she waited for her turn. She was too excited! For a moment, Martin Luther King stopped in front of her. His gaze was steady, and he looked right into her eyes. She put out her hand and smiled. He took her hand firmly in his and smiled back.

*Martin Luther King, Jr., speaks to a group of
young people about civil rights.*

"She still talks about it," Jones said to a reporter recently. "She remembers it to this day."

Reverend Jones left First United Methodist in 1963. A new youth minister took his place. Well, not quite. No one could replace Don Jones. Hillary kept in touch with him after he left. Once she wrote, "The new minister thinks I'm a radical."

But Hillary didn't waste much time worrying about what the new youth minister thought of her. By 1964 she was thinking about college. While most of her classmates wanted to stay close to home, Hillary was looking east.

Two favorite teachers pointed her toward Wellesley College in Massachusetts. She also considered Radcliffe and Smith. All were women's colleges.

"She was set on going to an all-girls school," said her mother.

Her teachers pushed her hard to look beyond the small town of Park Ridge. And when she was accepted at Wellesley, they helped her work out the financial aid she would need.

Hillary was a popular and active student at Main South High School. From clockwise top left, she is shown with other participants on a TV quiz show, with the National Merit Finalists, with Student Council Representatives, and with the Student Council Committee Chairmen.

Hillary smiles for her first-year photo at Wellesley College.

"They were both so bright and smart and such terrific teachers, and they lobbied me so hard to apply to schools I had never thought of before. So I went to Wellesley."

Her parents drove her to Massachusetts. She must have been thrilled, but her mom didn't share her excitement.

"Hillary hadn't really been away from home, and when she went to Wellesley, it was really, really hard. After we dropped her off, I just crawled in the back seat and cried the eight hundred miles home."

Hillary may have been homesick, but she didn't waste any time before getting involved in college politics. She jumped right into the middle of an ugly controversy in her freshman year at Wellesley.

4

Working Things Out

The tension in the hall was electric. A meeting of the entire college had been called over a question of race. Should more black students be admitted to Wellesley? Black women already attended the college, but in small numbers. They believed that Wellesley actively tried to keep down the numbers of black students admitted each year. They were angry and demanded change.

"But why should they come here for nothing, when my parents pay to send me?" some of the white students complained. They were

34

angry because many minority students got financial aid.

Suddenly a young woman stood up to plead for more minority admissions. Some students booed and jeered. The woman broke into tears.

It was an emotional debate. But Hillary went calmly from group to group encouraging people to keep talking.

"We've got to talk. We've got to work things out. It's the only way we can solve this problem."

And students listened.

Finally someone called out, "Let's vote! We need a vote!"

Everyone voted. It was resolved that more minority students should be admitted to Wellesley. In time, Hillary became head of the civil rights organization on campus.

"Hillary was definitely one of a handful of leaders," says a friend who was a class-

*Black demonstrators in Alabama are sprayed
with powerful jets of water by the police.*

mate. "She was the one who was always giving speeches, calling meetings, making things happen."

Another friend remembers that "she was always so enthusiastic, that she inspired other people to follow her."

And it seemed that not only Wellesley but also the country needed leaders. Gathered around their dorm TV's, Hillary and her friends felt they were watching their world disintegrate. In horror, they saw police turn dogs and water hoses on peaceful Freedom Marchers across the South. On college campuses around the country, students just like them demonstrated against the war in Vietnam. But the war went on, and demonstrations got angrier, and sometimes students got

Hillary probably watched clashes like this one between military police and anti-war protesters on television.

Hillary relaxes with friends.

into battles with the police. These violent images impressed the young Hillary.

But she wasn't all work and no play. She

knew how to have fun. When asked what they love and remember about Hillary, friends often talk about her sense of humor and wonderful laugh. In college, she went to football games and parties. She danced a lot, mostly to songs by the Beatles and the Supremes. And she continued to keep close friendships with men as well as with women.

She dated, but didn't spend much time in front of the mirror. As a classmate recalls, "She was not a woman who spent a lot of time thinking about how she looked or what she wore."

"Hillary was never style-conscious," her mom once said. "She didn't need to have what her friends had. I think she thought makeup was superficial and silly when she was younger."

Then in April of 1968, tragedy struck.

Hillary's roommate was studying in their dorm room the day Dr. Martin Luther King,

Martin Luther King, Jr., and followers, including Jesse Jackson, stand on a balcony at a hotel in Memphis, Tennessee, on the night before King is murdered.

Jr., was murdered. Suddenly, Hillary banged open the door. Books went crashing against the wall, and Hillary burst into tears. Her friend had never seen her so upset.

Hillary felt Dr. King's death personally. After all, she had met the man. She remembered his smile, and how warm and firm his handshake had been. Now he was dead! A great man murdered because he led the fight for racial justice! It was a long time before she could stop crying.

"It was that horrible event, more than anything, that firmed her resolve to do her utmost to stop injustice," said a friend.

On June 5, just two months after Dr. King's death, there was another terrible tragedy. Robert F. Kennedy, who was running for president and promising to end the war in Vietnam, was also shot and killed.

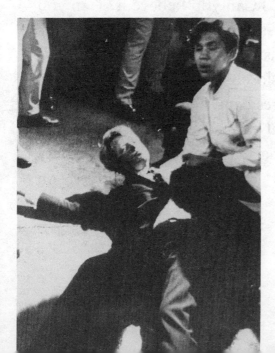

Bobby Kennedy lies on the floor moments after being shot.

Two great political leaders murdered in two months! What was happening in America? Hillary wanted to be the kind of person who could make things better. But how?

One way Hillary always felt she could make a difference was through student government. She had started out active in her freshman year. As a senior, she ran for president of the student government. It was a close race, but when the votes were counted, Hillary had won. In her excitement she turned to a favorite professor, grabbed his arm, and cried, "Can you believe it? Can you believe what just happened?"

Ruth Adams, then president of the college, worked closely with Hillary when she was student president. She once said of her, "She was not always easy to deal with if you were disagreeing with her. She could be very insistent." But though they disagreed on

42

Hillary shows her serious side during the student government elections for president at Wellesley.

many issues, says Adams, Hillary was never rude.

As graduation day approached, the students wanted a student to address them. So much had happened in their four years at Wellesley. But who could speak for all the different groups? Who could represent the

*On graduation day, Hillary talks with
college officials and Senator Brooke.*

blacks and the whites, the liberals and the
conservatives, the shy and the outspoken?

"There was no debate as far as I could

see," said Ruth Adams. "Miss Hillary Rodham, of course."

Hillary would share the stage with another speaker, Senator Edward Brooke. According to the schedule, he would speak first.

Graduation day arrived cool and clear. A sea of bright young women sat on the lawn facing the podium. Senator Brooke was introduced and delivered his speech. When he was finished, the parents gave him a standing ovation. But most students remained seated. A few clapped politely. Many sat in stony silence.

Eleanor Acheson, a close friend of Hillary's, said, "It was pretty much a canned speech. He did not weave into it what had happened to the country during the four years we were at Wellesley."

Senator Brooke hadn't said what they wanted to hear. Now it was up to Hillary.

When Hillary walked to the podium, it

was still so quiet only the rustling of her gown could be heard. She stepped up to the microphone. She paused a moment to look at her friends. Then classmates saw her set aside the speech she'd written. They looked sideways at each other and smiled. Hillary Rodham was about to stir things up. She spoke directly to Senator Brooke.

"We are not yet in positions of leadership and power," she began. "But our part is to question and criticize, and I find myself reacting to some of the things Senator Brooke said."

To Hillary it seemed that political leaders never talked about the important issues that challenged society. Senator Brooke had definitely not done it. So she decided to do the job in her speech.

Throughout her talk there were murmurs and gasps from parents, but cheers and clapping from students.

Hillary gives an exciting graduation speech.

She finished. This time the parents sat in silence, and it was the students who leapt to their feet and cheered!

One thing was clear. Hillary had won the love and respect of her friends and teachers.

Hillary poses outside against a beautiful New England background for her yearbook pictures.

One of her professors wrote of her: "She is by far the most outstanding young woman I have taught in my thirty years at Wellesley College."

After graduation, Hillary was going on to law school. Earlier in the year, when she was trying to decide between the law schools at Harvard and Yale, a friend introduced her to a Harvard professor: "This is my friend Hillary Rodham. She's deciding whether to come here next year or attend our closest competitor."

The professor was a tall man. He got up very slowly from his chair. He looked down at Hillary and said: "First, we don't have a close competitor. And second, we don't need any more women at Harvard."

If that was their attitude, Hillary thought, then she didn't need Harvard either! After graduating from Wellesley, she went to Yale Law School.

5

Meeting the Future

"And not only that, we grow the biggest watermelons in the world!"

Hillary turned to look at the young man who was speaking.

"Who's that?" she wondered out loud.

"That's Bill Clinton," said a friend sitting nearby. "And Arkansas is all he ever talks about."

Arkansas? thought Hillary as she looked again at the young man. Who would want to talk about Arkansas? It was the second poor-

Yale Law School

est state in the country. Hillary couldn't understand why anyone would want to go there, much less talk about it.

Bill Clinton had noticed Hillary, too. There were only a handful of women at Yale Law School. For that fact alone, Hillary would have been conspicuous. But like Bill, she was a star on campus. He was easy-going and popular. She was very smart, very sure of herself. And not afraid to speak her mind, as Bill would soon discover.

One night, in the Yale library, Hillary sat studying at one end of a long table. At the other end of the large study hall Bill Clinton was talking to someone. Or trying to.

Actually he was having a hard time paying attention because he had one eye on Hillary.

Hillary knew he was watching her. He had been practically following her for weeks now.

*The main reading room of the Yale Law School library,
where Hillary first met Bill Clinton.*

That's it, she thought. *Slam!* She shut her book. Then she marched the length of the library until she came face to face with Bill. He had been watching her come toward him like a tornado. He wasn't sure what was going to happen next.

*Hillary and Bill have always enjoyed talking about
ideas with each other. Here they share a laugh
at Hillary's tenth-year college reunion.*

"If you're going to keep staring at me,
and I'm going to keep staring back, I think
we should know each other. I'm Hillary Rodham. What's your name?"

Suddenly easy-going Bill went blank. For
a minute he forgot his name! They began
dating soon after.

They had similar ideas about using the law to help others. And Bill had a vision. He was heading back to his home state of Arkansas. He had plans to run for governor. Hillary wasn't as sure about her future. She was as deeply involved in school issues at Yale as she had been at Wellesley. She helped edit a legal journal, studied hard, and worked with poor children at the medical school's hospital. But what exactly she would do after Yale wasn't clear.

In the spring of 1970 Hillary was scanning the main bulletin board on campus. Lectures and events were posted there. In one corner she saw a small notice for an upcoming lecture by Marian Wright Edelman. Hillary knew about her work on behalf of the poor. Marian was a black woman skilled in civil rights law. Hillary was looking forward to hearing her speak.

That evening, she slipped into the back of

Hillary and Marian Wright Edelman, seated far right, still work very closely together on issues concerning children and families.

the lecture hall. She heard Marian tell the audience: Use your education for the good of the poor. You have a responsibility to help others.

This is exactly what Hillary wanted to

hear. When Marian finished, Hillary walked up and introduced herself. She told Marian she wanted to work for her during Yale's summer break. The older woman welcomed the enthusiastic student but said, "I have no money to pay you."

"That's okay," said Hillary. "Find me a job, and I'll find the money."

And she did find the money. She got a Yale grant to work with Marian's organization. That organization would later become known as the Children's Defense Fund.

Her job was to talk to migrant workers and their families, the same kind of people she had helped as a teenager in Park Ridge. She was to find out what kind of education, if any, their children got. Did they get medical care? She especially wanted to understand the suffering of the children in the camps. How did they live in a place where there was no running water or electricity?

When Hillary returned to Yale, she knew her future work would be with children and their families. She was concerned with the plight of poor and abused children. Her vision was taking shape. But would she go on alone or share her life with Bill?

After graduating, Bill went back to Arkansas. He asked Hillary to come with him, but she wasn't ready. She took a job in Washington, D.C. She joined the staff of special counsel John Doar. Doar's job was to look at the charges against President Nixon during the Watergate scandal.

Hillary called her Washington experience "one of the greatest personal and professional opportunities I've ever had."

She had been on Doar's staff for only eight months when President Nixon resigned. That meant their work was finished. She could go back to work with Marian Edelman, but Bill still wanted her with him.

Bill Clinton signs papers as a young attorney general for Arkansas.

Should she follow her heart to Arkansas or pursue a career in law on her own?

She spoke with many of her friends. They all had different opinions. But in the end

Hillary was the one who had to decide. Her heart won. Bill was there to meet her when she arrived at the Little Rock airport.

Hillary landed a job teaching law at the University of Arkansas. A year later, on October 11, 1975, she and Bill were married in a small ceremony for family and a few close friends. At first they claimed that they didn't have enough time for a honeymoon. Her mother said, "Nonsense!" and got cheap tickets for Bill, Hillary, and the whole Rodham family to go to Acapulco, Mexico.

"We had a marvelous time!" said her dad, Hugh, Sr.

Most of Hillary's friends thought she had moved to Mars. Arkansas seemed as far away as that, and almost as alien. Hillary could have gone into politics and maybe someday come back to Washington as a senator, they said, or even a Supreme Court justice! She could have gone to New York City and become a rich corporate lawyer. Instead, she went to Arkansas. It seemed she was following Bill's dream, not her own.

Hillary practiced law in Arkansas. She became a partner in a nationally known law firm in Little Rock. Despite that, friends still thought the move was a waste of her amazing talents. They should have known Hillary better. Arkansas, it turned out, would become her training ground for the White House.

6

First Lady of Arkansas

"Thank you! Thank you!" Bill Clinton yelled, waving to his enthusiastic, cheering supporters. His dream had come true! In 1978 he was elected governor of Arkansas. At 32 years of age he was the youngest governor in America.

In Arkansas, governors serve two-year terms. Bill and Hillary had so much they wanted to do in those two years. So many problems needed solving. Problems in education, health care, and the environment. Bill

The Arkansas State Capitol Building

was young and idealistic. He wanted to fix everything right away. Many people came to mistake Bill's excitement and energy for arrogance. It felt as if he was always telling folks what *he* thought *they* ought to do. Over the years, Hillary had become his chief adviser. He turned to her for advice, but she was having problems of her own.

Unlike most wives, Hillary had not taken Bill's name when they married. She still called herself Hillary Rodham. Arkansas is a conservative state, and many people were angry. Why wasn't she Hillary Clinton?

And she also continued to practice law, even though she was Arkansas's First Lady. Why wasn't she back at the Governor's Mansion instead of at her law office? Sometimes reporters didn't know where to find her.

Of course, Hillary did many things the wives of governors are expected to do. She raised funds for local hospitals. She attended 4-H farm shows. But her stubborn streak of independence bothered people. They wanted someone more traditional as First Lady of the state. The people of Arkansas were not happy with the young couple in the Governor's Mansion.

One bright spot was the birth of Chelsea, her "one perfect child," as Hillary has called her.

Once, when Chelsea was four weeks old and had been crying for hours, Hillary said to her, "Chelsea, you've never been a baby before, and I've never been a mother before. We are just going to have to help each other get through this."

As a new mom, she spent as much time as possible with her baby. She had promised herself that Chelsea would always be the most important thing in her life. But taking care of a new baby as well as being a lawyer took lots of time. She was often too tired to help Bill as much as she had in the past. He missed her energy and advice.

When Bill ran for re-election in 1980, he lost. Voters thought he was too pushy and

*Proud parents Hillary and Bill show off
newborn baby Chelsea.*

Hillary was too different. She was an outspoken wife who had kept her own name. There had been criticism about her style of clothing and her big glasses. People thought she looked unattractive and didn't care about looking nice. Hillary was confused about how to respond. She had always felt that what you thought and did was more important than how you looked.

Both Bill and Hillary took the loss hard. But they had learned something important. They discovered that while change was necessary, it couldn't be pushed on people.

They didn't give up. Bill planned to run again in 1982.

But first, Hillary decided she needed to make some changes of her own. One of the first things she did was take her husband's last name. Now she was Hillary Clinton. Her name change actually made headlines!

When people wanted to know if Bill had

*Hillary and Bill get back on track to becoming
the First Couple of Arkansas once again.*

asked her to do it, she said, "He's probably
the only person in Arkansas who hasn't!"

She told a reporter, "I just decided that it

was not a big issue to me when it came right down to it."

People had complained about her baggy clothes. So she got a new wardrobe. She cut her hair to shoulder length. And she replaced her big glasses with contacts.

In 1982, Bill was re-elected governor of Arkansas. At a triumphant inaugural ball, the band played "Happy Days Are Here Again," a famous old Democratic Party theme song. And they *were* happy days for the Clintons. But Bill and Hillary still had changes planned. Hillary was especially eager to tackle big problems in the schools.

Bill appointed her to head a committee that would look at the schools and make suggestions for change. Hillary was about to spark one of the biggest political battles in the state's history.

She traveled all over Arkansas. She talked to parents and teachers in open town meetings. She discovered that parents did want better schools but did not know how to make changes. Hillary began to make a list of what they wanted. After hours, days, and weeks of listening she drew up a plan.

One part of the plan was to have teachers take tests to make sure they were good teachers. Just the way kids had to take tests to show they were good students.

Another part was a program to help children develop learning skills before they went to school. She got the idea from an article in a Miami paper. Excitedly, she ripped it out and called a friend.

"Listen to this!" she said. "Let's see if we can do it in Arkansas."

The idea was to prepare poor mothers to teach their toddlers at home. The mothers taught them about shapes and sounds and played special games with them. When the children entered kindergarten, they were ready to learn. The mothers in the program were proud. Helping their children learn made them feel good about themselves.

However, neither of these changes was easy to make. The proposal to test teachers was very unpopular. Teachers were insulted and angry. "Why should *we* have to take tests?" they cried. And not everyone thought a program to help poor moms teach their children would work.

Hillary's skills as a negotiator helped her work through a tough situation. She listened to everyone's concerns. Parents had told her the changes they wanted to see in the schools. And they got those changes because Hillary stuck to her goals.

Bill and Hillary Clinton were in the Arkansas governor's mansion for ten years. They were good, productive years. But now Bill was ready to realize an even bigger dream. From the time he was a teenager he

The Clintons visit the White House in 1986.

had cherished the dream of running for president.

When he was a high school student, he had even met President Kennedy. Like

Kennedy, he wanted to make a difference, not just in his state, but in the country.

Bill and Hillary felt ready for the challenge of a presidential race. And they finally felt Chelsea was ready. Several years before they had considered a run for the presidency but then decided against it. Chelsea was too young, they thought. But now their daughter was twelve years old. A presidential campaign would be tough, but she would stay in Little Rock with Hillary's parents, who had moved there from Park Ridge to help out. She would continue to go to school, and they would try to keep her life as normal as possible—even though circumstances would be far from normal.

One day in 1991 Hillary sat down to write a letter to a Wellesley professor and friend. No public announcement of their plans had been made yet, but she wrote: "We are about to begin a great adventure."

The first months of the campaign were difficult for Hillary and Bill. Here a serious Hillary listens to her husband deliver a speech.

7

The Campaign Trail

It was March 1992, many months into the presidential campaign. Hillary Clinton stood outside a Chicago bakery. The campaign had begun in great excitement, but now things were getting nasty. Several candidates wanted to win their party's nomination for president. Cruel things were said about everyone, but especially about Hillary. Newspaper and magazine reporters followed her everywhere, asking irritating questions. She had gone through a governor's campaign in Arkansas. But nothing could have prepared her for this.

"Mrs. Clinton! Mrs. Clinton!" yelled the reporters, pushing to get closer.

On this chilly, windy day at the Chicago bakery she was campaigning for her husband. Flashbulbs exploded as she spoke to the store owner.

Recent articles had accused Hillary of getting state cases for her law firm because her husband was governor. Didn't the law firm where she worked have an unfair advantage? Didn't that mean *she* had handled cases for the state that had made her a lot of money?

No, she said. "I have done everything I knew to do to be as careful as possible, including turning my back on funds that were coming into my firm from the state."

Hillary was furious. She was particularly angry about a comment suggesting she should not have even worked outside the governor's mansion while she was First Lady of Arkansas. Then she made the statement that would haunt her for the rest of the campaign.

"I suppose I could have stayed home and baked cookies, but I decided to pursue a career of my own."

When people heard this, they were outraged. Especially homemakers. What was wrong with staying home and baking cookies? But they hadn't heard Hillary's entire statement. The truth was, she had gone on to say: "The work I've done has been aimed to assure that women can make the choices they want to make, whether it's a full-time career or full-time motherhood."

Hillary Clinton was fast becoming unpopular. Reporters were writing about the "Hillary Problem." She was a symbol of the '90s woman. A woman who wanted to have it all. A wife, mother, and lawyer, active and outspoken, and certainly not traditional.

Many people didn't feel ready for all the changes Hillary seemed to stand for.

Some people will make fun of those they don't understand or who make them uncomfortable. Reporters began making fun of Hillary's clothes. Even her headbands! Other candidates for president criticized her. Even though it was Bill who was running for president, not Hillary!

Hillary Clinton had never cared how people looked. She cared about what they did with their lives. She felt that way about herself as well. This constant interest in what she wore and how she looked was hard for her to understand. She was hurt and confused by these attacks. But she believed that helping Bill get elected president, so that they could try to solve America's problems, was more important than dressing the way she pleased.

So she tried to turn the tide back in her

*Hillary continued her work for children
throughout the presidential campaign.*

favor. During the campaign she got rid of the
headbands. When she appeared with Bill, she
stood in the background rather than up
front. She loved to wear bold colors, but she
began to dress more conservatively. She even
got involved in a cookie-baking contest with
Barbara Bush!

*Hillary never let all the criticisms of her style
stop her from giving great speeches.*

People noticed the change. And some
thought she'd gone too far. One reporter
now wrote, "Please! Let Hillary be Hillary!"

She *was* still being Hillary, it just wasn't
being reported. She still gave electrifying

speeches to cheering supporters. She met with delegations from foreign countries, and with groups from around the nation. She shook hands and went to fund-raising dinners. And she also worried about Chelsea. How was her daughter handling all of this?

The Clintons made sure to keep doing things, like going to church, as a family during the campaign.

"When she was little, we told her that people in politics say mean things. Her eyes got big and she said, 'Why do they do that?' So far she's been able to maintain her own life."

Hillary describes herself as a "fanatic" mother. She helped Chelsea do homework by fax machine when she was on the road.

Her good friend Eleanor Acheson once remarked, "Hillary travels quite a bit. But after meetings break up or before a breakfast session begins, she always spends hours on the phone with Chelsea, discussing homework and a million different things."

When she wasn't with Chelsea or talking to her, Hillary was campaigning for her husband. She had made a few surface changes for people, but mostly she went her own way. She knew people would have to decide for themselves whether they liked her or not. She didn't feel she could do much to change their minds. She could get rid of her head-bands, but she wouldn't stop being herself.

By the end of that summer Hillary was back on top. Voters had grown tired of the unkind stories. They liked the fact that Hillary never attacked her critics. When friends urged her to respond by attacking back, she said, "Let's wait and see."

All the hard work becomes worthwhile for the Clintons and the Gores on Election Night, 1992.

"Hillary has a beautiful capacity to see the best in people," says her friend Carolyn Ellis. "I said to her once, 'You've hosted more teas than the rest of us will ever do in our lives. Why didn't you just come back and say that?'"

Hillary didn't say anything for a moment, then she replied, "That's not the way I want to be remembered at the end of my life."

On November 4, 1992, after a year of long, hard campaigning for her husband, Hillary Clinton became the First Lady-elect of the United States. She is now one of the most powerful people in the country. Maybe even in the world. How *does* she want to be remembered?

8

A New Kind of First Lady

Now that Hillary is First Lady of the land, what is she doing and how has she changed?

Well, she's dressing the way she's always enjoyed. She's wearing the bold colors she loves. Soon after the election she told the press she wanted the Rodham back in Hillary Clinton. Now she's Hillary Rodham Clinton. The first First Lady to use her maiden name *and* married name.

Soon after he took office, President Clinton appointed his wife head of the Health

*Hillary gives a happy thumbs-up at the lunch
following her husband's inauguration.*

Care Task Force. It was a huge job. Hillary
traveled across America, talking to patients,
nurses, and doctors. She oversaw hundreds

of people who helped her come up with a new health-care plan for America.

She has said, "I will make as much commotion as possible about issues important to the world."

She is the only First Lady to come to the job with so many degrees and so much professional job experience.

One reporter said of her, "She's really quite qualified to do anything she wants."

Hillary has often been compared to Eleanor Roosevelt. Eleanor was told more than once, "Stick to your knitting." That meant, Don't get involved in the men's work of government. The world wasn't yet ready for a First Lady who was powerful in her own right. But Eleanor ignored the criticism. It was the time of the Great Depression. People were out of work and hungry. She used her position to bring attention to the suffering she saw around her. And though President Roosevelt often asked her to be his "eyes and ears," he wasn't always supportive of her activism. They did not work together as closely as Bill and Hillary Clinton in making political decisions.

President Clinton openly admires his wife's abilities. She has a great partnership with him. Staffers have often heard the President say "Run it by Hillary" when there is a question about a decision.

She was there when he met with members of Congress for the first time as president.

Afterward, he told reporters, "She knew more about some of these issues than we did."

This is a couple that works together. Hillary was deeply involved in choosing people for the Cabinet. Cabinet members are close advisers to the president. As head of the Heath Care Task Force, she often met with members of Congress to discuss the plan she

*The First Lady has met with many members of Congress
to discuss her new health-care plan.*

was trying to craft for the country.

But in the spring of 1993, while she was trying to help others solve their health-care problems, her father suffered a stroke. Hillary canceled all her meetings and flew immediately to the hospital. Chelsea went with her. On the plane ride to Little Rock, Chelsea and Hillary worried about Hugh, Sr. They tried to think about the good times they had enjoyed with Hillary's dad. They talked about Christmas parties, birthdays, and softball games.

For several weeks Hillary didn't do any work on health-care reform. She did not attend meetings or take calls. Twelve hours a day she sat by her father's hospital bed.

But Hugh, Sr., was too sick to survive the stroke. He died several weeks later. There was little time for Hillary to be alone after his death. The job of being First Lady, in charge of health-care reform, couldn't wait any longer. There wasn't much time for grieving.

Although some people hold onto the image of a First Lady as a stay-at-home wife and mom, this is not the reality of women's lives in the '90s. Most wives and mothers work.

Eleanor McGovern is the wife of another governor who also once ran for president. She told a reporter: "Hillary Clinton is the new woman. Not everyone has kept pace with the idea of today's professional woman. I think it's going to take some getting used to. But I think it's good for the country to have a First Lady like that. Maybe it'll help us grow up a bit."

First Ladies used to work "behind the scenes." Not Hillary. Of course, she will talk privately with the president, but already her role and her power are quite public. No matter what Hillary Rodham Clinton does for

*A bold new look for Hillary Rodham Clinton
as she moves into the future with big plans.*

the rest of her husband's term, she has
already changed the role of First Lady for-
ever.

Who knows? If we can get used to a powerful First Lady, we might actually elect a
woman as president!

VALERIE SPAIN is an author and artist who enjoys writing about important women in American culture. She lives in the Boston area with her husband, two sons, two cats, and a gerbil.

Bullseye Biographies

Meet Hillary Rodham Clinton ✓
Meet Jim Henson
Meet John F. Kennedy
Meet Martin Luther King, Jr. ✓
Meet Shaquille O'Neal
Meet Steven Spielberg
Meet Oprah Winfrey ✓